The Little
All Through

Activities for each season

by Lorraine Frankish

Illustrations by Martha Hardy

LITTLE BOOKS WITH BIG IDEAS

Published 2009 by A&C Black Publishers Limited
36 Soho Square, London W1D 3QY
www.acblack.com

First published by Featherstone Education, 2007

ISBN 9781-1-905019-748

Printed in Great Britain by Latimer Trend & Company Limited.

This book is produced using paper that is made from wood grown in
managed, sustainable forests. It is natural, renewable and recyclable.

The logging and manufacturing processes conform to the environmental
regulations of the country of origin.

**To see our full range of titles
visit www.acblack.com**

Contents

Introduction

This Little Book of activities for all times of the year complements **The Little Book of the Seasons** by offering additional activities for young children which reflect the changing year. **The Little Book of All Through the Year** contains ideas for walks, visits and outdoor activities, most of which can be offered in your garden, outdoor area or local park if you are located in a city.

In addition to these physical activities, the book offers ideas for art, craft and technology explorations on seasonal themes, and a wide range of simple and healthy foods to make and eat together, so even your snack times can have a seasonal flavour.

The activities are suitable for children aged from three to seven, although the younger ones may need more help. As usual, the book encourages independent learning and exploration, giving children opportunities to explore preparing their own foods, growing their own vegetables, collecting their own art and collage materials, sorting and looking closely at familiar objects, and recording what they find in words, pictures, sounds and individual creations.

Seasonal changes provide perfect opportunities to plan activities for early

learning, encouraging children to become more aware of the changes in their environment. **The Little Book of All Through the Year** aims to promote an awareness of the many changes that take place each year. The activities are designed to help children to recognise the changing patterns in nature, the weather and temperature. Playing outdoors is obviously the best way to do this.

This can be in a large, rural or landscaped area or a small modest space in a city or town.

Whatever your setting, children need to learn through their senses, smelling fresh flowers or damp logs, feeling the wind or soft rain on their face, listening to birdsong or leaves rustling in the trees, looking up at a dark and cloudy sky, or playing in the shade while the sun creates shadows. They also need to taste fresh tomatoes they've grown themselves, gather natural collections and use these for activities and investigations indoors to extend their understanding.

Although most of the recipes included can be made at any time of year, they are set out to make the most of food that is naturally available at a given time. This not only means that ingredients should be at their best and cheapest, but will also provide further opportunities for children to be more in tune with the seasons.

Young children may not immediately be aware of subtle differences and changes in their environment, but the activities are intended to capture their interest at a level they can appreciate. From this early start, encouraging and supporting them to observe and investigate their environment through interesting, relevant activities will develop their sense of curiosity about their surroundings, giving them confidence to explore and make their own first-hand discoveries.

Most of the activities are about exploration and observation of the environment, comparisons and manipulation of natural objects, testing things out and carrying out simple problem-solving activities. You will find some key learning goals on each activity page, but as with all open-ended activities, you may find that the children take their learning in different ways from the ones you have intended. As with all early years activities, only the adult present at the time is able to identify the learning that actually goes on.

The Foundation Stage Curriculum Guidance states:

To give all children the best opportunity for developing effectively their Knowledge and Understanding of the World, practitioners should give particular attention to:

▶ activities based on first-hand experiences that encourage exploration, observation, problem solving, prediction, critical thinking, decision making and discussion;

▶ an environment with a wide range of activities indoors and outdoors that stimulate children's interest and curiosity;

▶ adult support in helping children record orally and in other ways.

And that effective learning involves:

▶ practical activities;

▶ interaction with each other and adults;

▶ opportunities to gather information;

▶ practitioners teaching powerful lessons by modelling different behaviours.

With regard to **Physical Development**, practitioners need to:

► provide a wide range of activities that give children the opportunity and motivation to practise manipulative skills, for example cooking and playing instruments;

► observe closely to establish the position in which children have the best control;

► teach children the skills they need, for example, cutting with scissors, and plan opportunities for them to practise those skills.

For effective **Creative Development**, practitioners should give particular attention to:

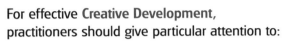

► a stimulating environment in which creativity, originality and expressiveness are valued;

► a wide range of activities that children can respond to by using many senses;

► sufficient time for children to explore, develop ideas and finish working at their ideas;

► opportunities for children to express ideas through a wide range of types of representation;

► physical contact with artefacts, materials, spaces and movements.

The activities in this book are intended to encourage independence where possible, with children taking an active part, using everyday equipment and with the emphasis on the process rather than any end result. Some of the activities do

have an element of risk – going out and about on walks, climbing into dark boxes and using kitchen equipment. It is important therefore to assess each individual child's abilities and level of understanding to gauge how much adult support and guidance they will need in order to be able to take on challenges, while still remaining safe.

Environmental awareness

Many of the activities also offer opportunities to develop a sense of care and feeling for conservation. Children may need to understand some basic rules for natural exploration, and some of these may be:

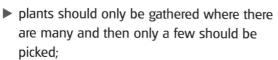

▶ plants should only be gathered where there are many and then only a few should be picked;

▶ plants and any other living things should be handled with care;

▶ where possible, animals should be observed in their natural environment and if removed for observation, should be returned quickly to the exact place where they were found.

Going Green, Growing Cress

After a spring walk, when children have noticed shoots on trees and plants, involve them in the process by growing some cress or beansprouts for a salad or some sandwiches for a home-grown snack.

What you need:

▶ cress or mustard seeds

▶ kitchen paper

▶ cotton wool

▶ clean empty yoghurt pots, one for each child

▶ tea spoons.

What you do

1. Give each child a yoghurt pot and show them how to scrunch up a sheet of kitchen paper and push it into their pot.

2. Use a dropper or small jug to add a few drops of water to the paper to dampen it.

3. Cover the kitchen paper with a thin layer of damp cotton wool, leaving about 2cm growing space between the top of the cotton wool and the top of the pot.

4. Sprinkle a few mustard or cress seeds on top of the cotton wool.

5. Press the seeds down lightly.

6. Leave the pots in a warm light place.

7. Check every day for signs of growth (sprouts should appear after about 5 days).

8. Make sure the seeds stay damp, using a hand spray.

9. Watch the seeds as they grow. Make drawings or take a photo sequence.

...and another thing

▶ Peel off the wrapper on the yoghurt pot and draw a face on the back using marker pens or poster paint. As the cress grows, it will look like hair.

▶ Grow bean sprouts by putting a few mung beans in a plastic jar, covering the top with muslin and securing with an elastic band. Dampen the seeds daily by filling the jar with water and then emptying it – the sprouts should be ready to eat in five to six days.

Key Goals for Learning

CLL   Extend their vocabulary, exploring the meanings and sounds of new words

KUW Find out about, and identify some features of, living things, objects and events they observe

CD   Use their imagination in art and design, music, dance, imaginative role-play and stories

Some key words

▶ seeds   ▶ photo
▶ grow   ▶ measure
▶ sow   ▶ shoot
▶ light   ▶ leaves
▶ water   ▶ roots
▶ today   ▶ cut
▶ tomorrow   ▶ sandwich

Stop, Look, Listen

Go for a walk to listen to the sounds of birds and look for signs of nest building. You could link this activity to exploring nesting materials, making nests and ICT work in recording and reproducing birdsong. You don't have to live in the country, just visit a park, city farm, nature reserve or garden.

What you need:

▶ suitable clothing and footwear for walks

▶ cameras, tape recorders and binoculars

▶ clipboards and pens or pencils

▶ carrier bags for collecting nesting materials

▶ materials for nest building (wool, string, ribbon, twigs, sticks, grass, hay, leaves and feathers etc.)

▶ reference books and other sources for bird recognition.

What you do

1. Plan a simple walk, with some points of interest and possible areas to stop and listen. Don't forget to carry out a risk assessment of the route before you go, and get the necessary permissions from parents.

2. Persuade as many adults as possible to join you on this walk. Small groups will allow children to listen carefully and talk about what they hear.

3. Before setting off with the children, ask them to think about what sounds they might hear and look at picture books of birds nesting.

4. Along the walk, stop and stand quietly for a short time, without talking. Listen! Then talk about what the children can hear.

5. Listen again and then ask if they can hear birdsong. Can they see where the birds are? Look up in the trees or in hedges for nests or nesting materials. Use binoculars to help find the birds.

6. Try recording some birdsong, or taking photos of nests and birds.

7. Collect some nesting materials – sticks, twigs, dry grass and moss for nest building later.

...and another thing

▶ Take a notepad on the walk and list the sounds. Encourage the children to describe the sounds – draw pictures and simple words (even made-up words) to discuss later.

▶ Take small binoculars for a closer look at what is in the trees.

▶ Help the birds with their nest building – cut strips from materials, such as string, wool and fabrics, and place them outside where birds can find them.

▶ Try making nests from natural materials (bird or child size).

Key Goals for Learning

PSED Maintain attention, concentrate and sit quietly when appropriate

CLL Sustain attentive listening, responding to what they have heard by relevant comments, questions or actions

CD Respond in a variety of ways to what they see, hear, smell, touch and feel

Some key words

▶ listen	▶ loud
▶ quiet	▶ cheep
▶ hear	▶ twitter
▶ nest	▶ build
▶ feathers	▶ weave
▶ song	▶ beak

Puddles

Whenever it rains, puddles form in low places, bringing many opportunities for measuring, predicting and calculating. Above all, children just love jumping in puddles, so make sure you have plenty of protective clothing and footwear for this springtime activity.

What you need:

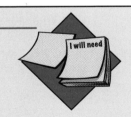

▶ suitable clothing and footwear for wet weather

▶ chalk

▶ meter measuring stick or tape measure (optional) – you could make a measuring stick from a broom handle or a cane marked with coloured lines or in sections

▶ a camera.

What you do

1. Involve the children in watching the weather forecast and the local signs for rainy weather. Be ready to go at a moment's notice!

2. After it has rained, go outdoors to look for puddles in your outdoor area, or in the park or local area.

3. Walk around the area and count the puddles.

4. Look carefully at each to see if you can tell how deep they are. Use a measuring stick to measure depth and distance across each puddle. You could walk through the puddles and count the steps for each, or stand in the middle and mark the water level on the children's boots.

5. When the children have had a good splash in the puddles, you could explore evaporation. Draw a chalk line around some puddles and return later to see if any of the water has evaporated. Keep drawing lines as the puddle evaporates. Talk about what is happening.

...and another thing

▶ Give the puddles names or numbers and monitor each puddle, comparing the sizes of different puddles. Do puddles always appear in the same places in your garden? Talk about why this might be.

▶ Give the children decorator's paintbrushes so they can use the puddle water to paint with and watch as their marks evaporate.

▶ Make wet tracks by walking or riding wheeled toys through shallow puddles and onto dry areas.

Key Goals for Learning

PSRN Use language such as 'greater' or 'smaller' to compare two numbers or quantities
Use language such as 'bigger' to describe the shape and size of solids and flat shapes

PD Move with confidence, imagination and in safety

Some key words

▶ puddles
▶ measure
▶ depth
▶ diameter
▶ evaporate
▶ splash

▶ boots
▶ waterproof
▶ tracks
▶ round
▶ across
▶ dry

Green Stuff

Making a green leaf salad will involve children in tasting many varieties of leaves, and draw their attention to other leaves and shoots that are appearing in the environment. You could even grow your own salads in growbags, tubs or window boxes.

What you need:

▶ a variety of salad leaves

▶ 200ml water

▶ 200ml olive oil

▶ 55ml white vinegar

▶ 1 teaspoon of mixed herbs (or 1 tablespoon of fresh herbs).

What you do

1. You can make a good and varied leaf salad from a bag of Baby Leaf or Continental salad from a supermarket, but it's better to grow your own or visit a greengrocer to get different sorts of lettuce and other salad leaves.

2. Wash the leaves and let them dry.

3. Spread the leaves out on a clean surface so that the children can look at them and compare size, shape, colour, texture and taste.

4. When they have looked at them, let the children shred the larger leaves into pieces.

5. Put all the leaves in a bowl.

6. Make a basic salad dressing by mixing all the remaining ingredients together.

7. Pour a little dressing over the salad and mix before eating.

...and another thing

▶ Try growing lettuce from seed. Use a large trough or tub of compost, or a growbag. Sprinkle the seeds in the compost and water well. The seedlings should begin to sprout within 7 to 14 days time.

▶ Do some leaf printing with different sized leaves (remind the children that not all leaves are edible).

▶ Take apart a whole lettuce, such as an iceberg. Count the leaves and note how the whole lettuce has become many different pieces.

Key Goals for Learning

KUW Look closely at similarities, differences, patterns and change
Find out about, and identify some features of, living things, objects and events they observe

CD Explore colour, texture, shape, form and space in two and three dimensions

Some key words

▶ green	▶ like
▶ leaf	▶ salad
▶ leaves	▶ shape
▶ whole	▶ size
▶ taste	▶ colour
▶ flavour	▶ pattern
▶ different	

Rhubarb, Rhubarb

Rhubarb is available in shops at this time, but as it is easy to grow, some families may have it in their gardens and may offer it free.

Don't use or let children handle the leaves of rhubarb as they are poisonous!

What you need:

- 4 sticks of rhubarb
- 1 tablespoon of water
- 4 tablespoon of caster sugar
- 110g margarine or butter
- 110g demerara sugar
- 180 – 200g flour
- serrated knives
- oven tray
- ovenproof dish
- chopping boards or clean surface for chopping.

You could use a supermarket crumble mix instead of making your own.

Safety Note:
Remove the leaves before children handle the rhubarb. The leaves are poisonous.

What you do

1. Preheat the oven to 180°C/350°F/Gas Mark 4.

2. Wash the sticks of rhubarb and cut them in half using a serrated knife. Help those children who need it.

3. Cut them into chunks about 3cm long.

4. Place on an oven tray and sprinkle with the water and caster sugar.

5. Place in the oven for about 10 minutes until cooked. Or cover with cling film and cook in a microwave for about 2 minutes.

6. Put the cooked rhubarb in an ovenproof dish.

7. Put the margarine, flour and sugar in a bowl and show the children how to rub it between their fingertips till it looks like fine breadcrumbs.

8. Sprinkle the topping over the rhubarb.

9. Bake in the oven for about 40 minutes.

10. Remove and allow to cool slightly before putting into individual dishes.

11. Talk about how the rhubarb has changed and is soft, and that the topping is now crunchy.

...and another thing

► Add other ingredients to the crumble topping, such as porridge oats, Weetabix or a little cinnamon. Talk about texture and smell as well as taste.

► Make a rhubarb pie by cooking the rhubarb as above, and roll out enough pastry to cover the fruit. Bake for about 30 minutes.

► Prepare and cook the rhubarb and serve with custard.

Key Goals for Learning

PSRN In practical activities and discussion begin to use the vocabulary involved in adding and subtracting

KUW Look closely at similarities, differences, patterns and change

KPD Move with control and coordination

Some key words

► rhubarb	► fingers
► sprinkle	► cook
► crumble	► hot
► crunchy	► sweet
► top	► sour

Cheesy Cauliflower

Getting children used to eating vegetables is a task for us all!
Making your own food is a good way of encouraging children to try new
foods and understand what goes into meals. This is a quick and easy
version of a traditional dish, and children can do most of the preparation.

What you need:

- ▶ one cauliflower
- ▶ 150g grated cheese
- ▶ vegetable knives (knives with rounded ends are safest) and forks
- ▶ a clean board or cutting surface
- ▶ a colander
- ▶ a saucepan and lid
- ▶ four small bowls.

What you do

1. Collect the equipment and the ingredients on a clean surface.

2. Look at the whole cauliflower together and talk about the shape, size, weight and the difference between the outer leaves and the centre.

3. Cut the cauliflower into quarters to provide a flat base. This will help the children to do the rest of the cutting. You could use forks to hold the pieces of cauliflower steady while cutting.

4. Help the children to cut the cauliflower into smaller florets. Talk about what you can see now. Look at the flower shape of the pieces.

5. Wash the pieces and drain in a colander.

6. Cook in a saucepan of boiling water, with a lid on the pan, for 4 – 5 minutes, until the pieces are just tender.

7. Drain immediately and when cooled slightly, divide into four separate bowls.

8. Add half the cheese to the cauliflower and mix with a fork.

9. Sprinkle the rest of the cheese on the top.

10. Put under a grill to melt the cheese.

...and another thing

As an alternative, add a white sauce to the cauliflower. You could use a supermarket packet mix or make your own from: 25g butter or margarine, 25g plain flour, 600ml/1 pint milk. Melt the butter in a saucepan. Stir in the flour and cook for 1 – 2 minutes. Take the pan off the heat and gradually stir in the milk to get a smooth sauce. Return to the heat and stir all the time. Bring to the boil. Simmer gently for 8 – 10 minutes. Cheese can be added to this sauce, which can also be added to pasta, pizzas and other vegetables.

Try chopping cauliflower and other vegetables to eat raw for a tasty snack or with a dip.

Use cauliflower florets to make interesting additions to vegetable printing activities.

Key Goals for Learning

PSED Select and use activities and resources independently

PSRN Use language such as 'more' or 'less', 'greater' or 'smaller' and 'heavier' or 'lighter', to compare two numbers or quantities

Some key words

- ▶ cauliflower
- ▶ florets
- ▶ colander
- ▶ half
- ▶ sprinkle
- ▶ melt
- ▶ cheese
- ▶ grate
- ▶ knife
- ▶ shape
- ▶ fork
- ▶ sauce

A Colour Walk

With preparation, a short walk can get children really looking at colours in their surroundings, noticing nature and making decisions about whether colours are the same or different and how they change over time as the seasons change.

What you need:

▶ the garden of your setting or a local park, field or nature area

▶ shade cards from a DIY store or decorator's shop (or put 'colour wheel' or 'paint colours' in Google to find lots of different shade cards)

▶ pieces of card (about 10cm x 20cm) for experiments with paint shades

▶ ready-mixed paint in primary colours, plus white and black

▶ pallettes, bun tins, plastic egg boxes etc. for mixing paint

▶ brushes, small spoons and plastic droppers for paint.

I will need

What you do

This activity is best if you have a discussion, a walk or outside experience, then explore colour mixing and matching. You could offer this activity outside, or make paint shade cards and then take them outside for matching with natural colours.

1. Prepare for a seasonal colour walk by talking about what you might see and the colours that may be around. You could tell a seasonal story from a picture book with a seasonal theme, or look at some nature books that cover seasons. Talk about the different times of year and why certain colours are linked to each season (greens and yellows for spring, reds and sky blues for summer, orange, brown and yellow for autumn, and white, grey and cold blues for winter).

2. Take the children out of doors and look for the seasonal colours in your garden or neighbourhood. Talk about what you see.

3. When you get back, look at the range of paints and brushes you have. Younger children might have more success with a restricted palette of colours suited to the season.

4. Help the children to mix the paints together in palettes to make different colours and shades, painting stripes or blobs of each shade on a card as they make them.

5. When dry, let the children take the colour cards outdoors and look for natural objects that match the colours on their cards.

...and another thing

▶ Gather grasses, petals and leaves, and mix paints to match the colours. Use the paint and natural materials for a summer picture.

▶ Using paint shade cards from DIY stores, go on a colour match walk. Choose cards that have similar colours to those present in the garden at the time of the activity.

Key Goals for Learning

KUW Find out about, and identify some features of, and living things, objects and events they observe

CD Explore colour, texture, shape, form and space in two and three dimensions

Some key words

▶ colour   ▶ tones
▶ names   ▶ pastels
▶ mix   ▶ same
▶ match   ▶ different
▶ shades

Blooming Marvellous

Drying petals and flowers will involve children in seeing changes and provide a natural resource for many art and craft activities. If you haven't grown any flowers in your setting this year, ask parents, colleagues, friends and local gardeners to donate flowers and petals. Or try florists for 'end of life' flowers they can't sell.

What you need:

▶ petals, flowers and leaves – roses are especially good, but any flowers will do

▶ muslin or cotton fabric square approximately 10cm x 10cm

▶ newspaper

▶ a large tray

▶ magnifying glasses

▶ ribbon or string, small boxes or plastic trays and fragrance oil (optional).

What you do

1. Collect fallen petals or remove any faded heads from plants. If these are not readily available at the setting, ask parents to donate them.

2. Lay them out on a tray and feel, smell and touch them gently. Look closely – there may even be a few tiny insects among the petals.

3. Use magnifying glasses for a closer look, and look at whole flowers alongside their petals to see how they fit together.

4. Leave to dry out, turning them every day. This should take about a week depending on the thickness of the petals.

5. Pile the dried petals on a table or in a large bowl and explore them again, talking about the changes.

6. You can add a few drops of fragrance oil to the petals if you wish.

7. Put in individual containers, boxes, bowls for pot-pourri gifts or just to make your setting smell nice.

...and another thing

▶ Use dried petals for a fragrant collage. Use white glue and stick them on a transparent sheet of plastic for a lovely window hanging.

▶ Make rose petal tea. Rinse the fresh petals. Make up a pot of tea and sprinkle on rose petals. Let the tea cool before serving. Milk can be added if preferred.

▶ Put a few petals in small containers or ice cube trays, fill with water and freeze. Fill a water tray and float the ice. Watch it melt away to discover the petals.

Key Goals for Learning

KUW Investigate objects and materials by using all of their senses
Observe features in the place they live and the natural world

CD Respond in a variety of ways to what they see, hear, smell, touch and feel

Some key words

▶ petals
▶ flowers
▶ fragrance
▶ dried
▶ smell
▶ feel

▶ perfume
▶ crunchy
▶ smooth
▶ soft
▶ stick
▶ join

23

Summer Collections

Summer is the time when many children are out of doors more and seem to naturally collect things such as shells and pebbles. Making a feature of these treasures provides the opportunity to take a closer look at them, and handle and explore them in detail.

What you need:

► a large shallow cardboard box to fit 12 or 24 empty orange juice cartons

► PVA glue

► spreaders

► magnifying glasses

► collections of natural objects such as shells, pebbles, rocks, feathers, leaves, seeds and nuts.

I will need

Safety Note:
Younger children may need adult supervision when working with small objects that may fit in ears or nostrils!

What you do

1. Cut off the tops of the cartons. Wash thoroughly and make sure they are really dry.

2. Put the cartons close together into the large box. You could glue them in place and to each other, but this makes them more difficult to empty.

3. Once dry, the cartons can be used to hold all sorts of natural collections. Help the children to collect objects to fill the different sections.

4. You could label the containers, but this may restrict the children's own ideas about how things could be sorted.

5. Talk with the children about the collections and then encourage them to handle and explore the objects you have collected.

6. Use magnifying glasses for closer examination.

7. The collections can be displayed in the large box on a table or fixed vertically to a wall.

...and another thing

▶ Use shoeboxes for displaying larger items, such as rocks or pine cones. Glue them together and leave on a table for sorting and exploring.

▶ Empty egg cartons, ice cube trays, chocolate box compartments, and bun tins are ideal to hold small items, such as pods or seeds. Offer the children small piles of things to sort into each compartment according to colour, texture, shape and size.

▶ Offer reference books and pictures so children can begin to identify seeds, leaves etc. for themselves.

▶ Extend your collections with man-made objects such as glass beads, fake jewels, sequins etc.

Key Goals for Learning

PSED Continue to be interested, excited and motivated to learn

CD Express and communicate ideas, thoughts and feelings using a widening range of materials

Some key words

▶ collection	▶ identify
▶ look	▶ sort
▶ explore	▶ same
▶ name	▶ different
▶ discover	▶ favourite

Making Waves

Empty plastic drinking bottles are in plentiful supply in the summer and can be used for many learning activities. This one involves children in making seaside bottles with summer objects. Make loads of bottles for loads of fun.

What you need:

► clear plastic drinks bottles with lids (small and large sizes)

► jugs, funnels and cups

► waterproof glue

► items to add to the water (see page 27)

► cellulose wallpaper paste to thicken the water (optional).

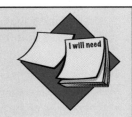
I will need

What you do

1. Wash the bottles thoroughly. Talk about what you are going to do and let the children choose which size bottle they want to use.

2. Help the children to fill their bottles with water, using jugs and funnels, till the bottles are about three quarters full.

3. Offer the children a selection of small objects to put in their bottles. Make sure they are small enough to fit through the necks of the bottles.

   These could include:
   food colouring or paint, glitter, sequins, small pieces of rolled up foil, trinkets, small pebbles, shells, beads, thin strips of plastic for seaweed and tiny fish shapes.

4. When the children have added the things they chose, top up the bottles with more water till they are almost full.

5. Put a little waterproof glue inside the lid and screw on to the bottle tightly.

6. When the bottles are dry, shake them and see what happens.

...and another thing

▶ Mix the food colourings to see what happens, or add bubbles.

▶ Add a little cellulose wallpaper paste to the water. This will thicken it and make the objects slow down.

▶ Fill bottles with sand instead of water, hold and move them to discover hidden objects such as beads and sequins or even small plastic minibeasts.

▶ Create underwater scenes, fantasy landscapes, snowscapes etc.

▶ Ziplock bags (available from supermarkets) can be used instead of bottles, but they may leak after enthusiastic handling!

Key Goals for Learning

KUW Investigate objects and materials by using all of their senses as appropriate

CD Use their imagination in art and design, music, dance, imaginative role-play and stories

Some key words

▶ shake	▶ careful
▶ move	▶ mix
▶ swirl	▶ waves
▶ sparkle	▶ storm
▶ colours	▶ snow
▶ pour	▶ leak

Fantastic Fans

Summers are getting hotter and sometimes we just need something to help cool down by moving the air. Make fans when the heat is on. The activity helps to develop hand and eye co-ordination and manipulative skills. Try all sorts of papers too – wrapping paper is a great alternative.

What you need:

▶ all sorts, colours and types of paper cut into A4 sizes

▶ felt pens or coloured pencils

▶ sticky tape or a stapler.

I will need

What you do

1. Using the felt tip pens or coloured pencils, decorate both sides of the paper. Wrapping papers will give lots of ideas for patterns and colour combinations.

2. Show the children how to make a fan by beginning at the short side of the paper and making a fold about 3cm wide.

3. Turn the paper over so that the folded part is underneath the rest of the sheet and fold back the edge again.

4. Repeat these two steps, folding and turning, until the entire sheet of paper is folded.

5. Hold one end of the folded paper firmly and fix at the end with sticky tape or a staple.

6. Holding the fixed end, open out the fan.

7. Flip your wrist rapidly to create a breeze.

8. Move the fan near your face to feel the air waft, moving your hair.

...and another thing

▶ While the fan is folded, cut out small pieces at intervals along the folded edge. Open up to reveal a pattern.

▶ Shake a sheet to create a much bigger breeze.

▶ Set up a discovery table with bought fans (hand and electric kinds) and try some out. Pin up the made fans close by for a stunning display.

▶ Cut out fish shapes from thin tissue or newspaper, put them on the floor and move them along by wafting the fans. Make this into a race.

Key Goals for Learning

PSRN Talk about, recognise and recreate simple patterns. Use everyday words to describe position

CD Handle tools safely and with increasing control

Some key words

▶ fold	▶ breeze
▶ press	▶ cool
▶ over	▶ hair
▶ underneath	▶ skin
▶ flip	▶ face
▶ waft	▶ feel

Chill Out

Fresh fruit or fruit juice ice lollies or milk lollies make a good alternative to drinks on hot days when children need to drink more.
Make these simple ice lollies with the children and leave them in the freezer to enjoy on a hot summer's day.

What you need:

▶ approximately 450g soft fruit such as banana, strawberry, mango or kiwi

▶ small quantity of fruit juice or water (optional)

▶ chopping board or clean surface

▶ vegetable knife (round ended knives are safer)

▶ a table knife and fork

▶ electric blender or potato masher

▶ ice lolly moulds and sticks – or yoghurt pots.

What you do

1. Wash the fruit thoroughly and peel if necessary.

2. Put the fruit on a chopping board or a clean surface. Talk about the different fruits and help the children to cut them into chunks.

3. Look at the difference in texture and shape, the smell, the juice and the seeds.

4. Put the fruit in a bowl and mash down with the potato masher, or blend with an electric blender.

5. When the fruit is fairly smooth, pour it into the moulds (you may need to add a small amount of fruit juice or water to make the puree liquid).

6. Freeze for about 90 minutes.

7. Push a lolly stick into each lolly and return to the freezer.

8. Leave to freeze overnight.

...and another thing

▶ For creamy lollies, mix half the fruit puree with yoghurt or crème fraiche, pour into the lolly mould and freeze for 90 minutes. Take the lollies out of the freezer and pour over the remainder of the fruit. Put in the lolly sticks and freeze overnight.

▶ Freeze pieces of fruit whole, defrost slightly before eating. Halved grapes, blueberries, raspberries and strawberries are good.

▶ Make lollies using orange or apple juice.

▶ Freeze berries in water in ice cube trays for a quick fruity refresher.

Key Goals for Learning

KUW Look closely at similarities, differences and patterns and change

Ask questions about why things happen and how things work

Find out about and identify the uses of everyday technology

PD Move with control and co-ordination

Some key words

▶ fruit names   ▶ chop
▶ peel   ▶ mash
▶ pips   ▶ blend
▶ seeds   ▶ freeze
▶ shape   ▶ ice
▶ outside   ▶ cold
▶ inside   ▶ favourite

Time for Tea

Scones are a traditional part of summer and are an essential for a real summer picnic. They are easy to make and children can do all the stages except the hot bit!

What you need:

- 225g self-raising flour
- pinch of salt
- 55g butter or margarine
- 25g caster sugar
- 150ml milk
- baking sheet
- mixing bowls
- tablespoons
- chopping board or surface

- 5cm round pastry cutters
- pastry brush
- oven gloves
- wire rack
- table knives
- butter and jam for serving.

I will need

What you do

1. Heat the oven to 220ºC, 425ºF, Gas Mark 7.
2. Gather the ingredients and equipment and read the recipe together.
3. Grease a baking sheet with a smear of the margarine/butter.
4. Mix together the flour and salt.
5. Show the children how to rub in the butter using their fingertips.
6. Stir in the sugar and then the milk to make a soft dough.
7. Sprinkle flour on the chopping board or surface.
8. Turn on to the floured surface and knead lightly.
9. Pat out the dough to form a circle about 2cm thick.
10. Use the cutter to cut out scones.
11. Place each scone on the baking sheet (makes about 8).
12. Bake for 12 – 15 minutes until well risen and golden.
13. Leave to cool on a wire rack.
14. Cut each scone in half and spread with butter and jam.

...and another thing

▶ Replace half the sugar with sultanas or chopped glacé cherries for fruit scones, or omit all the sugar and add grated cheese and a pinch of dry mustard for savoury scones.

▶ Have afternoon tea with strawberries and cream. Make it a special occasion and invite parents to join you.

▶ Make cakes and scones from playdough. Bake hard in an oven and use for a traditional café in the role-play area.

▶ Make several batches of the scones to sell at fund-raising events, or to make a novel Mother's Day gift.

Key Goals for Learning

CLL Use talk to organise, sequence and clarify events

PSRN Use language such as 'circle' or 'bigger' to describe shapes

PD Use a range of small equipment

Some key words

▶ scone	▶ mix
▶ sift	▶ bake
▶ rub	▶ hot
▶ pat	▶ cut
▶ measure	▶ spread

Our Own Tomatoes

Tomatoes are very good for children and adults. They contain vitamins and minerals and are even better for us after they have been cooked. Tomatoes are easy to grow from plants and always taste better home-grown.

What you need:

- ▶ young tomato plants
- ▶ large pots, tubs, growbags or hanging baskets (you can train the tomatoes up the chains)
- ▶ compost and gravel
- ▶ canes and garden ties
- ▶ small trowels and hand forks
- ▶ watering can and tomato fertiliser (optional).

What you do

1. If you are using pots, put some small stones in the bottom of a pot to improve drainage. Cover the stones with compost and fill the pot until it is about a third full. Follow the instructions when using a growbag.

2. Show the children how to carefully plant the little tomato plants in the compost, making sure the compost is firmly pressed down to help the plants stand firm.

3. Water the compost, then put the plants outside in a warm sunny place sheltered from the wind.

4. Water the plants every day, especially in hot weather. Add a little tomato fertiliser to the water once a week. Start to measure them as they grow.

5. As the plants grow taller and start to flower, push a cane into each pot and tie the stem to it. Talk about how the vine is getting bigger.

6. As the plants get bigger, note how they are growing up the canes.

7. Tomatoes can be picked when they begin to redden.

8. Harvest regularly to encourage more tomatoes to grow.

9. Talk about the distinctive smell, and taste the tomatoes at different stages of ripeness to compare flavours.

...and another thing

▶ Eat the tomatoes in salads or make simple chopped tomato salsa.

▶ Try making stuffed tomatoes: slice off the tops of whole tomatoes and scoop out the middles. Mix cooked rice and vegetables such as peas, diced pepper and sweetcorn together, and use these to fill the tomatoes. Bake until the tomatoes are soft.

▶ Make tomato sauce and use it to top ready-made pizza bases.

Key Goals for Learning

PSRN Use everyday words to describe position

PD Use a range of small and large equipment

Some key words

▶ tomato   ▶ vine
▶ plant   ▶ scoop
▶ compost   ▶ ripe
▶ cane   ▶ cook

Picnic Time

Take advantage of any nice day to have a surprise picnic in your garden or a local park. Keep the ingredients simple and involve the children in the preparation and choice of food for the picnic.

What you need:

▶ wet wipes, or napkins, plastic boxes, plastic or paper plates and cups

▶ picnic baskets, cool box with ice packs and a blanket or sheet

▶ fruit, water or juice

▶ for crusty French sticks:
French sticks, margarine, a teaspoon, small bowls, forks and a bread knife

Suggested fillings:
egg and cress, cheese and tomato, peanut butter and jelly, banana, tuna and mayonnaise (be aware of children with allergies)

▶ foil for wrapping.

I will need

Safety Note:
Picnic food should be eaten within two hours of preparation unless it is refrigerated.

What you do

1. Help the children to mix your chosen ingredients for a filling with a fork in a small bowl.

2. Cut the French sticks lengthwise in two.

3. Hollow out the centre of each stick with a teaspoon or clean fingers and put in the bowl with the filling. Mix together and pack back into the bottom part of the stick. Cut the stick into short lengths and wrap the whole stick in foil or cling film.

4. Wash any fruit you are taking and chop larger fruit into smaller pieces.

5. Don't forget drinks!

6. Together, pack everything into baskets or bags, so the children can help with carrying.

7. Carry the picnic basket outdoors together and find a shady spot.

8. Spread out your blanket and share the food you have prepared.

...and another thing

▶ Cut pitta breads in half and fill, or spread fillings on a tortilla wrap.

▶ Make sandwiches together.

▶ When it's too wet to sit outside, lay a blanket on the floor and have an indoor picnic.

▶ Take teddies and soft toys along for a teddy bear's picnic.

▶ For a special picnic, plan ahead and invite parents to come along.

▶ Make any snack time into a special occasion by taking it outside, even on wet days, by rigging up an awning or erecting a tent or two.

▶ Planning and preparing picnics gives good practice for list-making.

Key Goals for Learning

PSRN Use mathematical ideas and methods to solve problems

KUW Select the tools and techniques they need to shape, assemble and join materials

Some key words

▶ picnic
▶ basket
▶ pack
▶ hollow
▶ napkins

▶ carry
▶ spread
▶ shade
▶ share
▶ favourite

Rainbow Fruit

Exploring and preparing a range of fruits involves making comparisons, talking about flavours, colours and shapes, and the benefits of a healthy diet. These activities will help children to explore and taste new foods.

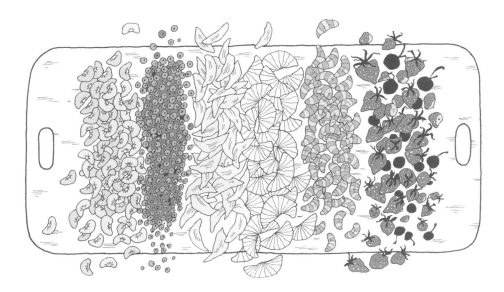

What you need:

► a variety of fruit such as water and other melons, strawberries, pineapples, mangoes, kiwis, oranges, red and green grapes, apples and bananas

► knives suitable for children (round-ended and not too sharp)

► dessert knives and forks

► chopping boards.

I will need

What you do

1. Children may need assistance with some of the fruits. Younger children will be able to chop soft fruit, such as banana or kiwi, with a table knife. Those using a vegetable knife will find it easier and safer to hold the fruit in place on the chopping board with a fork. Name the fruit and talk about the smell, colour, size, texture, weight and shape. Look at markings, skins, peel and stalks.

2. Wash the fruit thoroughly and peel if necessary.

3. Place the fruit on a chopping board and help the children to cut the fruit into thick wedges or slices.

4. As they work, discuss the difference in texture and shape, the smell, the juice and the seeds.

5. Talk about the different colours both of the peel and the inside of the fruit. Look for seeds and pips and collect these for other activities.

6. Place on a large dish roughly matching the colours of the rainbow (red, orange, yellow, green, blue, indigo and violet).

7. Enjoy eating the fruity rainbow together.

...and another thing

▶ Cut the fruit into small chunks and thread on to skewers to make kebabs.

▶ Use a melon baller and watch a large piece of melon change into lots of small balls.

▶ Cut up a colourful selection of vegetables, brush with a little oil and bake in a hot oven (220°C/425°F/Gas Mark 7) for about 40 minutes. Use red, yellow and green peppers, carrots, courgettes and aubergines. The roasted vegetables can be used as a pizza topping.

Key Goals for Learning

PD Recognise the importance of keeping healthy and those things which contribute to this

CD Explore colour, texture, shape that form in two and three dimensions

Some key words

▶ colours   ▶ pips
▶ fruit names   ▶ soft
▶ rainbow   ▶ crunchy
▶ peel   ▶ favourite
▶ seeds   ▶ taste

DIY Coleslaw

Many children eat supermarket coleslaw and using fresh ingredients will show them how it is made. It is a very economical food to make and can include a wide range of raw vegetables. The grating and chopping help fine motor control.

What you need:

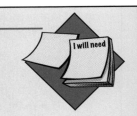

- ▶ 250g white cabbage
- ▶ 2 large carrots
- ▶ 4 spring onions
- ▶ 4 heaped tablespoons of bought mayonnaise
- ▶ knives suitable for child use and spoons
- ▶ chopping board or a clean chopping surface
- ▶ mixing bowls
- ▶ grater.

What you do

1. The children may not be able to slice the cabbage as finely as shop bought coleslaw, but this provides a talking point about the differences.
2. Look at the cabbage as a whole and talk about the shape, size and weight.
3. Cut the cabbage in half and look at the patterns inside. Take some photos of this stage and others.
4. Cut the cabbage into quarters.
5. Place the pieces of cabbage on a chopping board, flat side down.
6. Help the children to slice the cabbage into thin strips and place these in a big mixing bowl.
7. Grate the carrots and add them to the bowl. Chop the spring onions and add them.
8. Add mayonnaise a spoonful at a time, mixing between each spoonful. Continue to add mayonnaise until the consistency is right.
9. Eat in pitta breads or in sandwiches, or as a side dish with pizza or jacket potatoes.

...and another thing

▶ Try other varieties of cabbage, such as green sweetheart or red cabbage.

▶ Mix in other ingredients such as apple, celery, cucumber, broccoli florets, grated raw courgette, raisins or sultanas.

▶ Make your own dressing – mix together 3 tablespoons of fromage frais or natural yoghurt, 1 tablespoon of lemon juice and 1 teaspoon of honey.

▶ Make other salads, such as cubing cooked potato, adding a few chives and mixing with mayonnaise to create a potato salad.

▶ Print with cabbage sections to make interesting paintings.

Key Goals for Learning

PD Handle tools and objects safely and with increasing control

CD Explore colour, texture, shape, form and space in two and three dimensions

Some key words

▶ coleslaw
▶ vegetable names
▶ mayonnaise
▶ whole

▶ half
▶ quarter
▶ slice
▶ shred
▶ grate

A Real Pea Souper

This simple soup can be made all year round with frozen peas, but seeing fresh peas in a pod may be a new experience for some children. Peas taste nice straight from the pod too, and they are good for children.

What you need:

▶ 1 tablespoon of cooking oil

▶ 1 onion, finely chopped

▶ 500g fresh or frozen peas

▶ 1 litre of water or vegetable stock

▶ several sprigs of fresh mint

▶ colander, bowl, saucepan, electric blender or liquidiser.

I will need

What you do

1. Read the recipe together and put the equipment and ingredients in the order that you will need them.
2. Look at the pea pods and talk about their texture and shape and the feel of the peas inside.
3. Pop the pods by pressing on the join at the opposite end from the stalk. The pod should pop open showing the peas inside.
4. Push the peas out of the pod with thumb or finger and put in the colander.
5. Next look at the mint leaves. Talk about texture, smell and taste.
6. Tear the mint into smaller pieces.
7. Heat the oil in the saucepan and sauté the onions for 5 minutes.
8. Add the peas, water and mint.
9. Bring to the boil and simmer for 5 minutes.
10. Leave the soup to cool slightly and then blend it to a bright green soup.

Safety Note: Blending very hot soup is dangerous as it can force its way out of the top of the blender!

...and another thing

▶ Make croutons to float in the soup - remove the crusts from sliced bread and spread with margarine. Cut into cubes. Place on a tray and bake at 180°C, 350°F Gas mark 4 for 25 minutes.

▶ Soak dried peas in water overnight. Cut thin plastic drinking straws into smaller pieces and use to join the peas together to make sculptures.

▶ Go green for a week – have a green colour table, wear green clothes and make other green dishes – such as salads or green jelly.

Key Goals for Learning

PSED Be confident to try new activities

CLL Use talk to organise, sequence and clarify thinking and events

CD Explore colour, texture, shape, form and space

Some key words

▶ peas	▶ leaves
▶ pods	▶ cook
▶ shells	▶ soft
▶ inside	▶ pop
▶ mint	▶ smooth

Lemonade – The Real Thing

Make real lemonade – a refreshing drink that can easily be made from fresh ingredients. The recipe contains natural ingredients that will do no harm to the drinker!

What you need:

▶ 4 lemons

▶ 4 cups of cold water

▶ 1 cup of sugar

▶ citrus press, bowl, jug, knife and a chopping board.

What you do

1. Look at and handle the lemons together. Talk about the smell, colour, size, texture, weight and shape. Scratch the surface of the lemons to release the citrus oils.

2. Cut the lemons in half.

3. Put the citrus press in a bowl to catch the juice.

4. Put a lemon half on the citrus press and let the children turn it to squeeze the juice out. Some children may get better control if they stand up.

5. When all the lemons have been squeezed, pour the lemon juice into a jug.

6. Add the sugar and water to the juice in the jug.

7. Stir thoroughly until the sugar has dissolved. Taste to check sweetness and concentration. Add more sugar or more water if necessary.

8. Chill the lemonade or add ice cubes and enjoy a tangy drink.

...and another thing

▶ Use carbonated water for a fizzy lemonade.

▶ Make summer fruit drinks, combining two or three fruit juices together such as pineapple, orange, apple and cranberry. Add thin slices of fruit such as lemon and orange or a sprig of mint to make a tasty punch.

▶ Scoop out any remaining flesh and use the lemon skins to make lemon boats. Float them in a water tray. Fill with things to see how much they can carry, such as toy figures or animals, pebbles and shells.

▶ Draw a picture or pattern on a piece of white paper using a cotton bud soaked in lemon juice. When the juice has dried, iron the paper using a warm setting to reveal a brown picture.

Key Goals for Learning

PSRN Use language such as 'more' or 'less' to compare quantities

KUW Investigate objects and materials by using all of their senses as appropriate

Some key words

▶ lemon
▶ sweet
▶ peel
▶ bitter
▶ pith
▶ squeeze
▶ citrus
▶ taste
▶ sour
▶ smell

The Big Sleep

When it starts to get cold, some animals and insects go into a dormant state. A hedgehog hunt will provide an opportunity to talk about hibernation, as well as involving children in recognising numbers.

What you need:

▶ 10 soft toy hedgehogs (or other creatures that hibernate, such as frogs, bats, snakes, butterflies or ladybirds)

▶ number cards 1–10

▶ 10 white self-adhesive address labels

▶ a pile of fallen leaves (or leaves cut from paper).

What you do

1. Read a hibernation story, then talk about the change in the seasons and how and why some animals hibernate.

2. Help the children to write the numbers 1 to 10 on sticky labels and attach one to each hedgehog. Find or make some matching number cards.

3. Hide the hedgehogs in a pile of real or paper leaves in your garden or outdoor area (you could use smaller hedgehogs and a pile of leaves in an empty water or sand tray).

4. Look at the numbers on the cards and count each one to make sure the children are familiar with them.

5. Now hunt for the hidden hedgehogs.

6. As each hedgehog is found, ask what its number is and match it to the number card.

7. When all the hedgehogs have been found, put them in number order.

8. Count the hedgehogs from 1 to 10 again.

9. Find more hiding places for hedgehogs and continue the hunt.

...and another thing

▶ Look for hibernating insects under logs and leaves, but don't disturb them!

▶ Build a simple house for a hedgehog to hibernate in. Cut an entrance about 15cm in diameter. Put some shredded newspapers inside with clean, dry grass or straw on top and tuck the box near a hedge, if possible with the entrance facing south. Cover the top of the box with a small piece of plastic sheeting, for example, an opened up old carrier bag. Put twigs all round to make a dome and then cover with dry grass and leaves. Hopefully you'll get hedgehogs setting up home, but if not, the children will have enjoyed making a den.

Key Goals for Learning

PSED Work as part of a group or class

PSRN Recognise numerals 1 to 10

KUW Observe, find out about, and identify features in the place they live and the natural world

Some key words
▶ number names 1–10
▶ animal names
▶ season
▶ autumn
▶ hibernate
▶ winter
▶ sleep
▶ food
▶ cold

Spiders and Webs

The best time to see spiders' webs is early on an autumn morning, when they are noticeable, damp with dew, or during an early frost. Take some photos to add to an autumn display or a seasonal photo book.

What you need:

▶ magnifying glasses

▶ A4 black card

▶ hairspray.

I will need

What you do

1. Go outdoors searching for webs.
2. Look for more than one web as different spiders build different webs and no two webs look exactly the same.
3. When a web is found, make sure it is unoccupied. Study the intricate patterns and how it has been spun.
4. Notice where the web starts and how it is joined to bushes or objects.
5. Use a magnifying glass for a closer look.
6. Gently touch the web and talk about it being sticky to trap insects.
7. If you are sure the web is not occupied, spray a piece of black card with hair spray.
8. Hold the card behind an old web and gently pull the card towards the web so that it sticks to it. Take it inside to look at and display with web paintings.

Note: Some children have a genuine fear of spiders so be sensitive to their concerns.

...and another thing

► Read the story **The Very Busy Spider** by Eric Carle (Hamish Hamilton).

► Make paintings of webs, using black paper or card with silver or white paint or felt pens.

► Sing **Incey Wincey Spider**. Then put jugs, pipes, tubes and guttering in the water tray; add small plastic spiders and try flushing them through.

► Hammer nails into a log or flat piece of wood and thread wool or string around the nails to form a web pattern.

► Dance like spiders! Play music and crawl and hop around. Dance in ever-widening circles, spinning webs.

Key Goals for Learning

KUW Find out about and identify some features of living things, objects and events they observe

Observe, find out about and identify features in the place they live and the natural world

Some key words

► spider	► shiny
► web	► dew
► spun	► glisten
► thread	► catch
► intricate	► capture
► sticky	► pattern

Changing Seasons

As the days become cooler, leaves and seeds will be falling from the trees and children will be experiencing the changes in the weather. Taking photographs as a record of the changes will heighten their awareness of seasonal changes.

What you need:

▶ a camera

▶ outdoor place with a deciduous tree that sheds leaves in autumn.

What you do

1. Plan a simple walk to a place where there is a suitable tree or several different deciduous trees, such as a park, local wood or nature area.

2. Arrange to take plenty of adults, so children can talk and explore in small groups.

3. Before setting off, show the children the camera and how it works. Take more than one camera if you can borrow them, or invest in some cheap disposable cameras for the children to use. Take clip boards and pens to make notes and drawings.

4. Photograph the trees from several angles – at a distance, close up, looking up into the branches and down onto the ground. Don't forget to photograph the bark and leaves of each tree.

5. When you get back, look at the photographs and talk about the tree.

6. Revisit the same tree regularly until all the leaves have fallen, taking more photographs to discuss each time.

7. Display the photographs, or mount them in an album or scrapbook, in date order. Leave the photo book where children can look at it freely and talk about the changes.

...and another thing

▶ Jumble the photographs up and ask the children if they can arrange the pictures in the order of the seasons.

▶ Take photographs or a video of different areas outdoors throughout the year to prompt discussion. This could be presented as a Powerpoint presentation for children to revisit. Collect pictures and photos from home, magazines and websites depicting changes in the seasons.

Key Goals for Learning

KUW Find out about and identify the uses of everyday technology and use ICT to support learning

Observe, find out about and identify features in the place they live and the natural world

Some key words

▶ autumn   ▶ camera
▶ branch   ▶ photograph
▶ trunk   ▶ different
▶ leaf   ▶ shape
▶ fallen   ▶ colour

Leaf Match-up

Autumn is a great time to learn about trees and leaves. Visit your favourite trees again and, this time, look at the leaves of each one. Shape, colour and size are all mathematical concepts, so this is an opportunity to use them.

What you need:

▶ an area with a range of different trees

▶ suitable outdoor clothing

▶ bags for collecting leaves and seeds

▶ magnifying glasses, a camera and collecting bags.

I will need

What you do

1. Talk with the children and plan a simple walk, considering points of interest and possible areas to stop and look at different kinds of trees. You could draw maps together of the way you plan to go and what the children think they will see.

2. Keep to small groups of children for each walk, and take plenty of adults to help with looking and talking.

3. Go to the chosen area and find the trees. Touch the tree trunks and feel the bark.

4. Gaze up into the branches of the trees and watch them move in the wind. Notice leaves falling down from the trees.

5. Gather a pile of leaves and choose one each.

6. Run round the area to find someone else who has a similar leaf. The match could be by kind, shape, colour or size.

7. When a match has been found, stand together until everyone has found a match. Now play again.

8. You could play the same game with seeds and nuts if you find these.

...and another thing

▶ Pretend to be a tree – stand in a clear space, gently swaying in the wind. Stretch arms up high for branches. Someone walks around, pretending to be the wind and lightly touches each tree. When touched, the tree comes alive and bends and sways. Eventually everyone will be moving in a forest dance.

▶ Make a tree circle and hug a tree: stand around a tree trunk and hold hands. Move slowly round, maintaining the circle.

Key Goals for Learning

PSRN Talk about, recognise and recreate simple patterns

KUW Investigate objects and look closely at similarities, differences, patterns and change

Some key words
▶ leaf names   ▶ sway
▶ tree names   ▶ fall
▶ branch   ▶ drop
▶ twig   ▶ ground
▶ seeds   ▶ collect

Banana Curry

Bananas are a favourite fruit for most children and they are available all year round. This is a good recipe for a simple warm dish to eat as the days are getting colder.

What you need:

I will need

- 2 tablespoons of sunflower oil
- 1 teaspoon of chopped onion
- 1 garlic clove crushed
- 1 teaspoon of fresh ginger grated
- 1 teaspoon of curry powder
- 4 large bananas
- small carton of creamed coconut (available in supermarkets)

- vegetable knife
- grater
- saucepan
- teaspoons
- tablespoon
- table knives
- wooden spoon.

What you do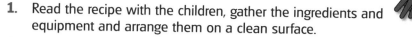

1. Read the recipe with the children, gather the ingredients and equipment and arrange them on a clean surface.

2. Peel the bananas, noting the differences of the skin and the flesh of the banana.

3. Touch and smell the garlic, ginger and curry powder.

4. Let the children chop the bananas into chunks using table knives.

5. In the saucepan, fry the garlic, onions and ginger in the oil until translucent, then add the curry powder and stir.

6. When the pan and contents are cool enough to touch, add the bananas.

7. Cover the bananas with the coconut milk.

8. Gently stir, but be careful not to stir too much as the bananas will break up easily.

9. Reheat until the curry is beginning to boil and then remove from the heat and leave to cool a little before serving.

10. Serve in small bowls on its own or with plain boiled rice. Encourage more reluctant children to taste just a tiny bit.

...and another thing

▶ Make your own curry powder. Grind the following spices in a blender or by hand in a mortar and pestle: 1 tablespoon of black peppercorns, 1 tablespoon of mustard seeds, 0.5 tablespoon of coriander seeds, 0.5 tablespoon of cumin seeds, 0.5 tablespoon of fennel seeds, 0.5 tablespoon of cayenne, 8 whole cloves. Store in an airtight container in the refrigerator.

▶ Move around the room like monkeys. When you hear the words: 'Bananas in Pyjamas', drop to the floor and pretend to be asleep.

Key Goals for Learning

CLL Know that print carries meaning and in English, is read from left to right and top to bottom

KUW Look closely at similarities, differences, patterns and change

PD Handle tools with increasing control

Some key words

▶ banana	▶ cook
▶ curry	▶ spicy
▶ garlic	▶ creamy
▶ peel	▶ tasty
▶ chop	▶ smell
▶ mix	▶ feel

Golden Lentil Soup

Red lentils are a striking orange colour although called red lentils. Children will be interested to see how the lentils change in colour and texture once cooked. They do not require soaking (unlike other lentils) and they cook quickly.

What you need:

- 1 large onion quartered
- 1 tablespoon of oil
- 225g split red lentils
- 650ml water
- large saucepan
- 1 teaspoon of salt
- a measuring jug
- curry powder or paste (optional)

- wooden spoons
- mixing bowl
- chopping board
- vegetable knives suitable for children
- electric blender
- kitchen scales.

What you do

1. Go through the recipe together and gather the ingredients and equipment you will need.
2. Put the ingredients and equipment in the order that they will be required.
3. Help the children to weigh out the lentils using the scales.
4. Put the lentils in a mixing bowl and talk about the colour and texture.
5. Put the onion pieces on a chopping board and help the children to roughly chop them.
6. Heat the oil in a fairly large saucepan and fry the onion for about 5 minutes, until it's lightly browned. You could add a bit of curry powder or paste.
7. Add the lentils, water and salt, and bring to the boil.
8. Simmer for about 15–20 minutes until soft and a brown colour.
9. When the soup has cooled slightly, blend to a fairly thick puree.
10. This soup tastes good with wholemeal bread or rolls, and is a great warmer after an autumn walk.

...and another thing

▶ Fill a bowl or pet tray with red, green or brown lentils, and provide scoops and bowls for the children to play with.

▶ Go on a colour hunt together and search out anything that is orange.

▶ Play Ready, Steady, Cook and make up recipes with only orange ingredients, such as oranges, mandarins, peaches, apricots, cantaloupe, mangoes, nectarines, carrots, pumpkins, sweet potatoes, squash, baked beans and marmalade. You might even have a go at making some of their suggestions!

Key Goals for Learning

CLL Know that print carries meaning

KUW Look closely at similarities, differences, patterns and change

PD Handle tools safely and with increasing control

Some key words

▶ lentils   ▶ smell
▶ orange   ▶ onion
▶ smooth   ▶ tasty
▶ blend   ▶ warm
▶ chop   ▶ favourite
▶ careful   ▶ taste

Apple Crisps

During the autumn, you may be offered apples by parents or others in the community who have plenty! Apple Crisps are chewy and sweet and are good to make with gifts or apples from shops or farm shops.

What you need:

- ▶ 4 eating apples
- ▶ margarine or oil for greasing trays
- ▶ chopping board
- ▶ vegetable knives suitable for children
- ▶ 2 baking trays
- ▶ oven gloves.

I will need

What you do

1. Look closely at the apples and at their similarities and differences. Look at shape, size, colour and texture of the skin.
2. Go through the recipe together and look at the equipment.
3. Look at the apple corer and talk about how it works.
4. Get the children to wash the apples thoroughly.
5. Put an apple on the chopping board and help the children to push the corer down through the apple on to the board.
6. Look at the cores and notice the pips inside (these are fun to plant and watch to see if they sprout).
7. Slice the cored apples in half (to make them easier to slice).
8. Place the flat side down on the board and slice the apple. Help those children who need it.
9. Put a thin layer of oil on the baking trays to stop the apples sticking.
10. Arrange the apple slices in a single layer on the trays.
11. Bake in the top of the oven for 20 to 30 minutes.
12. Remove from the oven and leave the apples to cool and become crispy.
13. Eat by themselves or with natural yoghurt.

...and another thing

▶ Apple printing is an old favourite. Remember to cut the apples from top to bottom and also around the circumference to create different patterns.

▶ Set up an interest table with different varieties of apples. Talk about the differences, such as shape, weight, size, colour, texture and taste.

▶ Visit a local orchard or a garden to see apples growing on the tree.

Key Goals for Learning

CLL Use talk to organise, sequence and clarify thinking, ideas, feelings and events

PD Recognise the importance of keeping healthy and those things that contribute to this

Some key words

▶ apples	▶ taste
▶ peel	▶ crunchy
▶ core	▶ soft
▶ corer	▶ raw
▶ pips	▶ cooked
▶ sweet	▶ grow

Baked Pumpkin

Don't just use a pumpkin for Halloween – use it to give cutting and cooking practice. Pumpkins are such an unusual vegetable, but are quite solid for young children to cut, so baking first makes them soft and easy to manage.

What you need:

- a medium sized pumpkin
- 4 tablespoons of butter/margarine
- cinnamon
- baking tray
- oven gloves

- baking foil
- 4 bowls
- 4 tablespoons
- 4 potato mashers
- 4 small dishes
- knife for cutting the pumpkin.

What you do

1. Preheat the oven to 350°F, 180°C, Gas Mark 4.

2. Examine the pumpkin as a whole and talk about how it looks, the ridges on the skin and the colour and texture of the skin.

3. Cut the whole pumpkin into quarters (do not peel it first).

4. Look at the inside of the pumpkin and talk about its smell and texture.

5. Scoop out the stringy pulp and seeds.

6. Put the seeds to one side for further activities.

7. Cover the pumpkin pieces with foil and bake for 1–2 hours until tender.

8. Leave to cool.

9. Help the children to scoop out the pumpkin using a tablespoon and put a portion in each mixing bowl.

10. Mash the pumpkin flesh using potato mashers, mix in the butter or margarine and a pinch of cinnamon, and continue mashing until the mixture is fairly smooth.

11. Serve in small dishes.

...and another thing

▶ Try adding different ingredients, such as natural yoghurt and honey to the baked pumpkin.

▶ Use the baked and mashed pumpkin in a pastry case for a pumpkin pie or to make into soup. Roast the pumpkin seeds and eat them, or use them for counting and sorting activities.

▶ Grow your own pumpkins. In the spring, seeds can be planted in peat or mushroom compost and will come up in two or three days on a windowsill to be later planted in the ground.

Key Goals for Learning

KUW Investigate objects and materials by using all of their senses as appropriate

PD Handle tools safely and with increasing control

Some key words

▶ pumpkin
▶ seeds
▶ orange
▶ foil
▶ shiny
▶ mash
▶ bake
▶ purée
▶ taste
▶ scoop

Blackberry Porridge

This is another colourful dish to make in the autumn when wild blackberries are freely available and ready for picking. If you can't find any near your setting, buy some or use other soft fruits such as raspberries or blueberries instead.

What you need:

▶ 2 medium sized eating apples

▶ 50g blackberries

▶ 100g porridge oats

▶ 8 tablespoons of natural yoghurt

▶ 8 tablespoons of water

▶ 4 teaspoons of runny honey

▶ grater, mixing spoons, mixing bowls and small bowls for serving.

What you do

1. Look closely at the different ingredients.

2. Grate the apples carefully.

3. Mix the oats, apples and berries together.

4. Notice how the porridge changes colour as it absorbs the juice from the blackberries or other berries.

5. Stir in the yoghurt and water.

6. Leave the porridge for about an hour. It can be left for longer, but you may need to add more yoghurt or water.

7. Stir in the honey.

8. Eat for breakfast, as a snack or as a healthy pudding.

...and another thing

▶ Make crispy granola with the same ingredients by using raisins instead of fresh fruit and mixing everything together with some vegetable oil till it begins to stick together. Spread thinly on a baking tray and bake in a low oven (gas mark 1, 275°F, 140°C) until golden brown. This can be served with yoghurt or as a topping for fresh fruit.

▶ Read **Goldilocks and the Three Bears**.

▶ Talk about porridge for breakfast. Ask the children to suggest ideas for breakfast and talk about their favourites.

Key Goals for Learning

PSED Select and use activities and resources independently

CLL Listen with enjoyment and respond to stories, songs and other music, rhymes and poems

KUW Look closely at similarities, differences, patterns and change

PD Recognise the importance of keeping healthy

Some key words

▶ blackberry
▶ porridge
▶ oats
▶ absorb
▶ honey
▶ mix
▶ stir

▶ sticky
▶ wait
▶ change
▶ taste
▶ spoon
▶ bears
▶ favourite

Guess the Seed

There are many ways seeds can be used in children's play to extend their learning and autumn is a good time to collect seeds and build on children's interest.

What you need:

▶ a collection of seeds: conkers, acorns, fir cones, sycamore helicopters – two of each kind

▶ a shallow cardboard box.

What you do

1. Before setting up any structured activities with conkers and other seeds that have been collected, allow the children plenty of time to explore and play with them in their own way.

2. Look at and talk about the seeds, spotting similarities and differences.

3. Put the cardboard box on its side on a table.

4. Put one of each of the different seeds in the box. Put the other seeds where all the children can see them.

5. Take turns to stand behind the box and choose one of the hidden seeds.

6. Without picking it up, describe the chosen seed.

7. The other children must try to guess which seed it is, and find the matching one from their side of the table.

...and another thing

▶ Bury some large seeds (fir cones, conkers, acorns) in the sand tray for children to hunt and hide again.

▶ Draw a grid in a tray of sand and play noughts and crosses with conkers and 'helicopters'.

▶ Put one of the seeds in a drawstring bag or box with a hole in the lid. Feel the hidden seed and try to guess which one it is.

▶ Grow your own tree! Half fill a plant pot with compost, place a conker or acorn on the soil and top up the pot with more compost. Leave it outside and water from time to time. Once the seed has germinated, keep it in the pot or plant in the ground.

▶ Make musical shakers by putting seeds in plastic film canisters.

Key Goals for Learning

PSED Maintain attention, concentrate and sit quietly
Work as part of a group or class, taking turns and sharing

KUW Find out about, and identify some features of objects they observe

CD Explore colour, texture and shape

Some key words

▶ seed names
▶ guess
▶ box
▶ tree
▶ soft
▶ hard
▶ smooth
▶ rough
▶ hide
▶ find
▶ match
▶ choose

Light and Dark

In the winter months, children will be getting up and going to bed when it is dark outside. Providing a dark place to hide and play in will focus their attention on this change and give them a lot of fun.

What you need:

► a large cardboard box – big enough for at least two children to sit in

► a fleece blanket or piece of soft fabric

► masking tape

► torches

► coloured cellophane

► elastic bands.

What you do

1. Lay a fleece blanket or some soft fabric inside the box to make a soft place to sit.

2. Use the masking tape to secure it in place if necessary.

3. Add some cushions if you have some.

4. Leave the box out for the children to play in freely. Some children may prefer to keep the box open, but for those children who want to make it darker, close the top down once they are inside, but make sure that they can get out when they want to!

5. Talk about light and dark and link this to night and day time.

6. Extend their play by offering them torches or safe battery lights to shine when they are inside the box.

7. Cut circles of cellophane and secure over the bulb end of some of the torches to create different coloured lights.

...and another thing

▶ Give the children some reflective clothing, such as Road Safety armbands or reflective waistcoats to test in the box. Shine the torches to make the light reflect (see Resources on page 84).

▶ Put some small objects inside a shoe or similar box and put the lid on. Cut a peephole in the side of the box so you can look at the objects.

▶ Make a peephole in a box, stick 'glow in the dark' shapes inside, and seal. Look at the shapes through the peephole. Take the lid off the box from time to time to let the shapes recharge in daylight.

Key Goals for Learning

PSED Have a developing awareness of their own and others' needs, views and feelings
Select and use activities and resources independently

KUW Talk about features they like and dislike

Some key words

▶ light
▶ dark
▶ day
▶ night
▶ inside
▶ outside

▶ hide
▶ shine
▶ colours
▶ scary
▶ brave
▶ soft

Let There be Light

As days become shorter, we use more electric light indoors and out. Making an electrical circuit is a good starting point to finding out about electricity. A film canister is a good size to hold and will produce a gentle glow.

What you need: (for each circuit)

▶ 4 (35mm) film canisters (free from most photographic shops)

▶ 4 Size C batteries

▶ sharp scissors or a bradawl

▶ 8 split pins

▶ 8 pieces of electrical wire approximately 15cm long

▶ a small bulb 6.6V/0.3amp (see Resources on page 84).

What you do

1. Prepare the canisters by piercing a small hole in the bottom and the lid of the canister with scissors or a bradawl.

2. Pull the split pins open wide so that they are flat.

3. Lay one end of each wire on them.

4. Fold the split pins together and push through the holes in the bottom and lid of the canister.

5. Open out the split pin inside the canister – this will secure the wire.

6. Wrap the other ends of the wire in a small piece of foil.

7. Place the battery into the film canister and push the lid on.

8. Form a circuit and make the bulb light up by putting one wire on the bottom of the bulb and one on the side.

...and another thing

▶ Talk about safety with regard to electrical sockets and plugs.

▶ Use an electricity science kit (from educational suppliers) and, with a higher voltage battery and a bulb holder, make a brighter light.

▶ Dismantle a torch so that the children begin to understand how it works. Then help the children to reassemble it.

▶ As most photographic shops will donate empty canisters, make use of them in other areas of the children's play:

   ▷ in sand and water trays
   ▷ outdoors for collecting and storing things
   ▷ filled with seeds to make musical shakers
   ▷ or for the children to use in their own creative way.

Key Goals for Learning

PSRN Use everyday words to describe position

KUW Build and construct with a wide range of objects, selecting appropriate resources, and adapting their work where necessary

Some key words

▶ electricity   ▶ fix
▶ battery   ▶ wire
▶ bulb   ▶ pins
▶ circuit   ▶ light up
▶ light   ▶ join
▶ container   ▶ together

Feed the Birds

Feeding birds and other wild animals in winter can be very rewarding for everyone in your setting, and will bring nature closer to the children, inspiring care and environmental awareness.

What you need:

- 4 empty yoghurt pots or margarine tubs
- 4 pieces of string approximately 25cm in length
- solid white vegetable fat (you will need 1 part fat to 2 parts bird seed)
- bird seed (available at garden centres and supermarkets)
- a big saucepan
- wooden spoons
- a mixing bowl.

Safety Note:
Some bird seed mixes contain nuts – check for children with nut allergies.

What you do

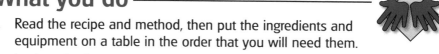

1. Read the recipe and method, then put the ingredients and equipment on a table in the order that you will need them.

2. Look at the fat in its solid state. Tip the bird seed into the bowl and explore it with fingers and eyes.

3. Melt the fat in a saucepan or microwave.

4. When it is cool enough but not solidifying again, gradually pour the fat into the bird food in the mixing bowl and stir well, taking turns.

5. Coil a piece of string into an empty yoghurt pot.

6. Spoon in some of the mixture.

7. Push the food firmly down into the pot, leaving the rest of the string sticking out of the top.

8. Leave the pots somewhere cold to set. When the fat has set hard, talk about how the ingredients have changed.

9. Remove the pots by dipping them in warm water for a second to help them slip off.

10. Talk about how the bird cake has taken on the shape of the pot.

11. Hang outside on a tree if possible, but in view of your windows.

...and another thing

▶ Use up stale bread and cereals by including these with the bird seed.

▶ Make a string of food to hang outside by threading hooped shaped cereal, such as Cheerios or Weetos, or peanuts in shells on to a string.

▶ Log the different birds that are attracted to the birdcake and look at books to identify the different species.

Key Goals for Learning

KUW Find out about, and identify some features of living things, objects and events they observe

Observe, find out about, and identify features in the place they live and the natural world

Some key words

▶ birds
▶ feed
▶ seeds
▶ solid
▶ soft
▶ mix

▶ melt
▶ stir
▶ press
▶ cold
▶ turn out
▶ hang

Keeping Warm

As the temperature drops outside and children need extra clothes to keep warm, here's a simple experiment to explore different ways of keeping things warm.

What you need:

▶ lidded boxes in different materials, such as cardboard, plastic and wood

▶ hay

▶ wood chip

▶ shredded paper

▶ 4 plastic drinks bottles.

What you do

1. Talk about keeping ourselves warm in winter and how we do that.
2. Half fill the boxes with the different materials.
3. Fill the plastic bottles with warm water.
4. Pass the bottles around and hold to check the temperature.
5. Place one warm bottle in each box.
6. Using the different materials, pack three boxes until they are full, making sure the bottles are in the middle.
7. Put one of the bottles unwrapped next to the boxes.
8. Put the lid on the boxes and leave for a while.
9. Check the bottles after about an hour to see if the children can feel any changes in temperature and to make comparisons of the bottles.
10. Return the bottles to the boxes and continue checking from time to time to note which bottle is cooling down quickest.
11. Run the experiments again, changing the kind of filling in each box to discover if this makes a difference. Try wrapping one of the bottles in foil, or a scarf or jumper.

...and another thing

▶ Carry out the above experiment using cooked food, such as pasta, to see if it stays warm and for how long.

▶ Put warm and cold drinks in vacuum flasks and cool boxes to check how they work and how long they maintain the temperature.

▶ Put a bowl of hand hot water and one of cold water from a fridge together on a table. Ask the children to put their hands in the bowls to discover how they feel and compare the differences. Have towels ready to dry hands.

Key Goals for Learning

KUW Ask questions about why things happen and how things work

PD Recognise the importance of keeping healthy and those things that contribute to this

Some key words

▶ temperature   ▶ hay
▶ warm   ▶ cosy
▶ cold   ▶ shreddings
▶ same   ▶ wool
▶ different   ▶ clothes

The Winter Collection

Gloves, hats and scarves come in so many different fabrics, bright colours and interesting patterns that children will be as interested in sorting them into categories as thinking about their purpose.

What you need:

- ▶ a large container, washing basket or box
- ▶ winter clothing such as coats, warm socks, hats and ear warmers
- ▶ pairs of gloves and socks
- ▶ equal number of scarves as hats.

What you do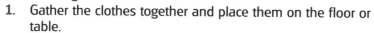

1. Gather the clothes together and place them on the floor or table.

2. Let the children explore the clothes, trying them on and talking about them.

3. When they have had plenty of time to explore the clothes in free play, begin to talk about the different sorts, patterns, shapes and sizes.

4. The children could sort the clothes into chosen categories, such as type of garment, colour or thickness.

5. Match up pairs of gloves or socks.

6. Take one pair of gloves and find a hat to match the colour.

7. Have a winter dressing-up race, where the children race to put on a hat, scarf, gloves, boots and a coat.

8. Talk about the clothes the children are wearing and how they keep them warm.

...and another thing

▶ Put a pile of pairs of mittens in the middle of the room. Ask each child to take one mitten. Play some music and ask them to dance and move.

When the music stops, ask them to find their matching mitten. Continue playing by taking off the mittens and putting them in the middle. Gloves can be used for this game, but some children will find it difficult to put them on and take them off quickly.

▶ Provide scraps of fleece, wools and other thick fabrics to make a winter collage.

▶ Put out small hats and gloves for use when dressing dolls and teddies.

▶ Look for matching patterns in clothes. Photograph the patterns close up and print pairs to make a pattern matching game.

Key Goals for Learning

PSED Dress and undress independently and manage their personal hygiene

KUW Look closely at similarities, differences, patterns and change

Some key words

▶ clothes ▶ thinner
▶ pattern ▶ warm
▶ texture ▶ pair
▶ thicker ▶ match

Juicing Pomegranates

Pomegranates are available from early to mid winter and as many children may not have seen or tasted one, now is a good time to try them. They need a bit of care in getting out the juicy pips, but they taste delicious.

What you need:

- ▶ 8 or more pomegranates (2 pomegranates produce one small cup of juice)
- ▶ a vegetable knife
- ▶ chopping board or clean work surface
- ▶ a skewer and a sieve
- ▶ tablespoons
- ▶ jugs for the juice
- ▶ plastic drinking cups.

What you do

1. Eating a pomegranate can be fiddly, as each pip has to be individually extracted, the juicy pulp eaten and the pips eaten or discarded. The pith is very bitter and unpleasant.

2. Juicing pomegranates is an easier way of tasting them.

3. Pass one pomegranate round so the children can look at and feel it together and talk about the leathery texture of the skin and the shape.

4. Slice this one in half using a vegetable knife to reveal the bright red and yellow fruit, and the seeds that create a star-like pattern. Let the children taste these by tipping a few onto a plate to pass round.

5. Now take turns with the other whole pomegranates. Roll them around the table top in every direction and press down to loosen up the juice inside.

6. Pierce the skin using a skewer or point of a vegetable knife to create a small hole. Older children could do this with help.

7. Using both hands, squeeze the fruit over the bowl to extract the juice.

8. Pour the juice into cups and taste.

...and another thing

▶ Buy some more juices (including pomegranate) from a supermarket for a tasting session. Make a chart of the favourites.

▶ Scrape all the fruit from the skins, leave to dry and then cut or tear into small pieces. Use the dry skins for gluing and sticking activities.

▶ Borrow a juicer and make other juices with carrots, tomatoes, oranges and berries. Make fruit juice lollies (see pages 30 and 44).

Key Goals for Learning

KUW Investigate objects and materials by using all of their senses as appropriate

PD Use a range of small and large equipment

Some key words

▶ pomegranate ▶ squeeze
▶ juice ▶ taste
▶ leathery ▶ like
▶ seeds ▶ favourite
▶ roll ▶ different

Parsnip Cake

Parsnips are sweet enough to put into a cake and this is a simple recipe to make together. Although it involves heating and baking, the children can still do much of the recipe independently.

Safety Note:
Fresh ginger is quite hot and should be handled by an adult.

What you need:

- 7 tablespoons plus 1 teaspoon of margarine
- 1 medium-sized or 2 small parsnips
- 2 cups of plain flour
- 1 teaspoon of baking powder
- 1 teaspoon of bicarbonate of soda
- 1 cup of sugar
- 1/3 cup of raisins
- half a teaspoon of salt

- 1 teaspoon of finely grated fresh ginger
- 1 teaspoon of ground cinnamon
- 1 cup of water
- 1 baking dish about 15cm x 32cm
- a large bowl and a hand held grater
- vegetable scrubbing brush
- 1 saucepan
- oven gloves, oven and hot ring.

What you do

1. Preheat the oven to 325ºF, 165ºC, Gas Mark 3.
2. Gather the ingredients and equipment and go through the recipe together.
3. Using 1 teaspoon of margarine, grease the baking dish.
4. Look at the parsnips and then scrub them with the vegetable brush.
5. Grate the parsnips using the fine holes of a grater.
6. Combine the flour, baking powder and baking soda in a large bowl and put to one side.
7. Put the margarine, raisins, sugar, salt, ginger, cinnamon and water in the saucepan.
8. Place over a medium heat and bring to a boil for about a minute, until the margarine has melted and the raisins are plumped.
9. Remove from the heat and leave to cool until tepid.
10. Pour this mixture into the flour and stir gently – just enough to moisten the dry ingredients.
11. Pour the batter into the prepared baking dish.
12. Bake in the oven for about 35 to 40 minutes until the edges of the cake start to pull away from the sides of the pan.
13. Remove from the oven and leave to cool.
14. Cut and serve, or wrap pieces in foil to take home.

...and another thing

▶ Parsnips can also be used to make soup or for roasting.

▶ Cut the tops off parsnips, and carrots too, and leave in a saucer of water to watch them sprout.

▶ Hide root vegetables in sand or compost for children to dig up and hide again.

Key Goals for Learning

PSED Work as part of a group or class, taking turns and sharing fairly

KUW Look closely at similarities, differences, patterns and change

Some key words

▶ ingredients ▶ bake
▶ grate ▶ share
▶ scrub ▶ cut
▶ tepid ▶ taste

Potato Wedges

Too many chips are evidently bad for children and adults. Here is a healthier version of fried chips as they are cooked in the oven. Making them in this way will also help children to be more aware of what chips are made from.

What you need:

I will need

▶ 4 medium potatoes, washed but unpeeled

▶ 2 tablespoons of vegetable oil

▶ pastry brushes and vegetable knives

▶ chopping board or clean surface

▶ baking tray, oven gloves, spatula and small plates.

What you do

1. Preheat the oven to 400°F, 200°C, Gas Mark 6.

2. Examine the potatoes carefully, looking at shape, colour, texture, weight, size, eyes and markings.

3. Place each potato on a chopping board and cut in half. Help children who need it.

4. Put the potato half flat side down on the chopping board and cut each half into wedges.

5. Brush a baking tray with some of the oil and put the potato wedges in the tray. Brush them with the rest of the oil.

6. Put the dish in the oven and bake for 25 minutes.

7. Take the dish out of the oven and turn the wedges over using the spatula.

8. Return to the oven for another 25 minutes until they are lightly browned.

9. Leave to cool slightly before eating.

...and another thing

▶ Find more wedge shapes – cheese, door wedges, wood blocks and shoe heels.

▶ Sing the song: 'One Potato, Two Potato...'.

▶ Explore other ways of eating potatoes – jacket, mashed (with other vegetables added), piped into duchess potatoes, sliced and baked etc.

▶ Read **Oliver's Vegetables** by Vivian French together and talk about the vegetables he eats, including the potato chips, when he stays at his grandparents' house.

Key Goals for Learning

PSRN Use language such as 'bigger' to describe the shape and size of solids and flat shapes

PD Recognise the importance of keeping healthy and those things that contribute to this

Some key words

▶ wedge	▶ lumpy
▶ potato	▶ heavy
▶ brush	▶ careful
▶ bake	▶ slice
▶ crunchy	▶ wet
▶ colour	▶ smell

Cheese in a Stick

This simple recipe is an excellent way of developing hand and eye co-ordination. And celery is excellent for teeth and gum health.

What you need:

- ▶ 350g cream or other soft cheese
- ▶ 4 sticks of celery (taken from one head of celery)
- ▶ vegetable brushes
- ▶ bowls for washing the celery
- ▶ kitchen towels
- ▶ vegetable knives
- ▶ chopping boards
- ▶ small plates.

What you do

1. Before chopping the celery, look at the celery head and talk about the leaves and the base. Pull the sticks away from the head and look at individual sticks. Talk about the ridged texture, colour and smell. Look to see if there is any remaining soil.

2. Scrub each stick in water using the vegetable brushes.

3. Dry with kitchen towels.

4. Lay the sticks on a chopping board, hollow side down.

5. Using the vegetable knife, cut off any leaves. Help those who need it.

6. Chop each stick into about 3 pieces.

7. Turn the celery over and, using a table knife or butter knife, spread the cheese, filling the inside curve of each celery stick.

8. Arrange each filled stick on a plate or stand them in a mug.

...and another thing

▶ Sprinkle dried herbs into the cheese, such as chives or parsley, before spreading. Or add grated carrot or apple.

▶ Try other fillings, such as peanut butter (be aware of children with allergies) or avocado.

▶ Make a dip by adding a carton of natural yoghurt to the cheese. Chop celery and other vegetables for dippers.

▶ Fill a jar or vase with water and add some food colouring. Put a few sticks of celery in the coloured water and leave them to absorb the dye. The celery will slowly draw up the coloured water. This will take between 6 and 12 hours. Cut a celery stick in half to reveal the veins filled with colour. Try the same experiment with a white carnation.

Key Goals for Learning

PSRN Use language such as 'bigger' to describe the shape and size of solids and flat shapes

PD Recognise the importance of keeping healthy and those things that contribute to this

Some key words

▶ ingredients
▶ equipment
▶ chop
▶ spread
▶ fill
▶ curve
▶ taste
▶ crunchy
▶ favourite
▶ help

83

Resources

Oliver's Vegetables; **Vivian French; Hodder Children's Books**

Oliver's Fruit Salad; **Vivian French; Hodder Children's Books**

I Eat Vegetables; **Hannah Tofts; Zero to Ten**

I Eat Fruit; Hannah Tofts; **Zero to Ten**

Autumn Nature Activities for Children; **Irmgard Kutsch; Floris Books**

Spring Nature Activities for Children; **Dagmar Israel; Floris Books**

Winter Nature Activities for Children; **Irmgard Kutsch; Floris Books**

Nature's Playground; **Fiona Danks; Frances Lincoln**

Earthwise Environmental Crafts; **Carol Petrash; Floris Books**

Time to Sleep; **Denise Fleming;**

The Easy way to Bird Recognition; **John Godley Kilbracken; Kingfisher**

1001 Bugs to Spot; **G Doherty; Usborne**

1001 Things to Spot in the Sea; **Katie Daynes; Usborne**

This is the Bear and the Picnic Lunch; **Sarah Hayes; Walker Books**

The Lighthouse Keeper's Picnic; **David Armitage; Scholastic**

The Giant Jam Sandwich; **John Vernon Lloyd; Macmillan Children's Books**

It's the Bear!; **Jez Alborough; Walker Books**

Other resources

Child's camera	Great Little Trading Company; www.glt.co.uk
	Fisher Price tough camera (Early Learning Centre); www.elc.co.uk
Reflective clothing	Three Bears Playthings; www.threebearsplaythings.co.uk
Electrical components	Commotion Group; www.commotiongroup.co.uk
Learning Through Landscapes	www.ltl.org.uk
Forest Schools	www.forestschools.com

* Prices correct at time of printing

The Little Books Club

There is always something in Little Books to help and inspire you. Packed full of lovely ideas, Little Books meet the need for exciting and practical activities that are fun to do, address the Early Learning Goals and can be followed in most settings. Everyone is a winner!

We publish 5 new Little Books a year. Little Books Club members receive each of these 5 books as soon as they are published for a reduced price. The subscription cost is £37.50 – a one off payment that buys the 5 new books for £7.50 instead of £8.99 each.

In addition to this, Little Books Club Members receive:
· Free postage and packing on anything ordered from the Featherstone catalogue
· A 15% discount voucher upon joining which can be used to buy any number of books from the Featherstone catalogue
· Members price of £7.50 on any additional Little Book purchased
· A regular, free newsletter dealing with club news, special offers and aspects of Early Years curriculum and practice
· All new Little Books on approval - return in good condition within 30 days and we'll refund the cost to your club account

Call 020 7440 2446 or email: littlebooks@acblack.com for an enrolment pack. Or download an application form from our website:

www.acblack.com/featherstone

Continuity and progression

The **Baby & Beyond**™ series takes simple activities or resources and shows how they can be used with children at each of the EYFS development stages, from birth to 60+ months. Each double page spread covers one activity, so you can see the progression at a glance.

Shows how simple resources can be used by children at different ages and stages

Inspiration for planning continuous provision

Messy Play	978-1-905019-58-8
The Natural World	978-1-905019-57-1
The Sensory World	978-1-905019-60-1
Sound and Music	978-1-905019-59-5
Mark Making	978-1-905019-78-6
Construction	978-1-905019-77-9
Dolls & Soft Toys	978-1-905019-80-9
Bikes, Prams, Pushchairs	978-1-905019-76-2
Role Play	978-1-906029-02-9
Finger Play & Rhymes	978-1-906029-01-2
Dens & Shelters	978-1-906029-03-6
Food	978-1-906029-04-3

To see the full range of Featherstone books visit www.acblack.com

through the EYFS

Ideal to support progression and extend learning.

Great for the Early Years Foundation Stage!

The **Little Books** series consists of:

All Through the Year

Bags, Boxes & Trays

Bricks and Boxes

Celebrations

Christmas

Circle Time

Clay and Malleable Materials

Clothes and Fabrics

Colour, Shape and Number

Cooking from Stories

Cooking Together

Counting

Dance

Dance, with music CD

Discovery Bottles

Dough

50

Fine Motor Skills

Fun on a Shoestring

Games with Sounds

Growing Things

ICT

Investigations

Junk Music

Language Fun

Light and Shadow

Listening

Living Things

Look and Listen

Making Books and Cards

Making Poetry

Mark Making

Maths Activities

Maths from Stories

Maths Songs and Games

Messy Play

Music

Nursery Rhymes

Outdoor Play

Outside in All Weathers

Parachute Play

Persona Dolls

Phonics

Playground Games

Prop Boxes for Role Play

Props for Writing

Puppet Making

Puppets in Stories

Resistant Materials

Role Play

Sand and Water

Science through Art

Scissor Skills

Sewing and Weaving

Small World Play

Sound Ideas

Storyboards

Storytelling

Seasons

Time and Money

Time and Place

Treasure Baskets

Treasureboxes

Tuff Spot Activities

Washing Lines

Writing

All available from

www.acblack.com/featherstone